Archbishop Daniel E. Pilarczyk

Living in the Lord
The Building Blocks of Spirituality

ST. ANTHONY
MESSENGER
PRESS

CINCINNATI, OHIO

Cover and book design by Julie Lonneman
ISBN 0-86716-155-8
Published by St. Anthony Messenger Press
Printed in the U.S.A.

Contents

Introduction: Saints Alive

In the Third Eucharistic Prayer of the Mass we pray to our God, "All life, all holiness comes from you through your Son, Jesus Christ our Lord, by the working of the Holy Spirit." That's what this book is about: life and holiness—our life and our holiness, the life and holiness that is in us through Christ Jesus by the working of the Holy Spirit. It is about Christian spirituality. It is offered by one who bears a teaching responsibility in the Church to people who are interested in living.

The fundamental reality of the life of Christian believers is that our life is no longer just our own life, but a sharing in the life of Christ. As St. Paul put it, "...I live, no longer I, but Christ lives in me..." (Galatians 2:20a). Jesus told his disciples that he was their life (see John 14:6). He assured them that they share his life just as the branches share the life of the vine (John 15:1-10). Consequently, when we speak about Christian living, we are not talking just about the life of an individual woman or man, but also about the life of the Lord Jesus, which somehow continues in and through those who have accepted him.

This life of Christ that is ours is not an abstraction, not merely a memory that we are supposed to revere and imitate. It is a real, true life, a life enlivened by the same Spirit that was in Jesus, a life that is prelude to something still more wonderful. "...[Y]ou are in the spirit if only the Spirit of God dwells in you," St. Paul says. "Whoever does not have the Spirit of Christ does not belong to him...If the Spirit of the one who raised Jesus from the dead dwells in you, the one who raised Christ from the dead will give life to your mortal bodies also, through his Spirit that dwells in you" (Romans 8:9b, 11).

Spirituality is the word that Christian tradition gives to the way in which individual believers, in practice, live out the life of Christ in the Spirit. Spirituality is not something that is peculiar to monks and hermits, but a fundamental element of the calling of every Christian believer. Spirituality answers the question: "What does it mean that Christ is living in me, here and now?"

There are some basics we need to grasp about spirituality if it is to be understandable to us.

First of all, spirituality is not a matter of acquiring something we don't already have or of becoming something we are not. Spirituality is rather a matter of being consistent with what God has already made us to be. Through faith and Baptism our God has given us the life of Christ. We don't deserve it. We can never make ourselves worthy of it. We can never earn it. It is a gift, pure and simple—a gift that is given to all those who have opened themselves to Christ.

This gift is the gift of holiness. *Holiness* is not a word with which we are very comfortable. We tend to associate it with those seemingly extraordinary women and men we call saints. It's not something we think applies to us. And yet it does. Holiness is nothing else than the life of Christ in us, the same life of Christ that was in the saints. They didn't make themselves holy and so win God's favor. They simply responded to what God had given them. In the same way, we don't become holy by following certain rules of behavior. We are holy through the gift of Christ's life in us.

God does not live in us like a tyrant, however, making us be and do what he wants regardless of our own inclinations. Rather, God comes to us in Christ and the Spirit as a guest, seeking a home in our lives.

Here lies the challenge of Christian spirituality. We are sinful men and women. We tend to be distracted by what is near at hand and to neglect what is really important in our lives. We find that rooting out bad habits and taking on good ones requires lots of time and effort, and so we are inclined to give up and just drift through life as we are. It seems much easier to put Christ into a back room of our lives, and spend most of our time and energy somewhere else.

Spirituality—living in the Lord, responding to the holiness that God has already given us—brings Christ out of the back room and into every aspect of our existence. It involves assimilating Christ into our real, concrete lives fully and completely. It is a matter of consistency, of integration, of living out in practice that which we already are. Living in the Lord means digesting, interiorizing, making freely and fully our own the life of the Lord Jesus which has been given to us. It means translating the life of Christ into our life so that it is at one and the same time authentically his and authentically ours. It's not an effortless process, to be sure, but neither is it an impossible one or one reserved for a chosen few.

It should be clear by now that living in the Lord is not just a matter of saying prayers or of having appropriate interior attitudes. The Christ whose life we read about in the Gospels was not concerned only with prayers and thoughts, but with life in the real world, in touch with real people. It is that life which we are called to share and to express. Consequently, living in the Lord has to do with our friends and our families, with our work and the life of our community, with marriage and achievement and suffering. There is no aspect of our human existence which is foreign to or separated from the life of Christ in us.

A complete treatise on Christian spirituality would deal with every conceivable aspect of human existence, because the life of Christ involves itself in some way in everything that is human. The reflections in these pages can only deal with a few such topics, but the basic truth remains: Living in the Lord has to do with living a human life, our life and his life. Nothing in human life is irrelevant to the life, the love, the presence, the holiness of Christ.

Sometimes people look on faith and religion as a harmless pastime for those who like such things, but without significant connection with "the real world." This is a mistake. In striving to live out the life of Christ, the believer is living in the same world as everybody else but is actually living there more realistically than the "realists."

Consciously or unconsciously, every human being wants to be happy. Happiness is what we are all striving for, one way or another. Happiness is a matter of expectation and fulfillment, of wanting and getting. The student studies to get a good grade in a test and is happy to succeed. The employee wants a better job with a bigger salary and is happy when it comes. People with unrealistic expectations spend most of their lives being unhappy because they never seem to get what they want. People who don't really know what they want just drift along, never really satisfied, never really fulfilled. Sometimes people actually get everything they want (or everything they think they want) only to find themselves restless and ill at ease because what they have chosen to pursue isn't really enough for them. But we are all motivated by desire. We all pursue some sort of happiness.

God has already given us as Christian believers everything that we could possibly desire. The satisfaction of every ultimate expectation is already ours in the life of Christ which we have been called to live. We have only to make that life our own, to let it permeate all that we are, to bring it forward into every aspect of our existence, to carry it into practice. Then real, final happiness is ours. That task is the agenda of our lives. That total acceptance of what God has made us to be is the pursuit of Christian spirituality, the pursuit of final fulfillment and true happiness. That's what it means to spend our lives living in the Lord.

For Discussion

1) If Jesus were not in your life, would it make any difference to the way you live?

2) What does "spirituality" mean to you?

3) What does holiness look like in the people you know?

Faith: The Focus

When we speak about living in the Lord it's important to get the fundamentals straight. It is true that living in the Lord is a simple thing: It means accepting for our own the life of the Lord Jesus which the Spirit has placed in us. But in order do that, we need to be aware of what is involved.

There are some basic realities that influence everything we do as participants in the life of Christ. Without them, living in the Lord is impossible. These realities are faith, hope and love. They are habits or qualities in our life that determine how we relate to God and, indeed, whether we relate to God at all.

These three basic qualities are all gifts of God. They are the fundamental elements that express the life of Christ in us. They are interrelated. In fact, they are dimensions of a single reality. It is possible to think of them and discuss them separately, but in practice we must be endowed with all three if we are going to live the life of Christ in any meaningful way.

Faith expresses the basic shape or form of life in Christ. Hope expresses the direction in which it moves. Love is the energy that keeps it alive. Here we will look more closely at faith, leaving hope and love for the following chapters.

The New Testament talks quite a bit about faith or belief. It is one of the main themes of the teaching of Jesus and his first followers. In the Gospel of John Jesus tells us: "This is the work of God, that you believe in the one he sent" (John 6:29b). At the tomb

7

of Lazarus Jesus tells Martha, "...[W]hoever believes in me, even if he dies, will live, and everyone who lives and believes in me will never die" (John 11:25b-26). Paul tells the Romans that the righteousness of God, that is, God's favor, comes "through faith in Jesus Christ for all who believe" (Romans 3:22b). The author of the Letter to the Hebrews says, "Faith is the realization of what is hoped for and evidence of things not seen" (Hebrews 11:1).

What are Jesus and his followers talking about when they speak of belief or faith in this way?

Faith consists in becoming aware that God is deeply in love with each of us and in responding to that love by making it the most important thing in our life. God's definitive approach to us is in Jesus, and so faith consists in accepting Jesus as the first and last word in human existence. Faith means giving ourselves to the Lord. Implicit in faith are attitudes such as recognition, trust, obedience, assent, acknowledgment. But the bottom line is form or focus. By faith we determine what the shape of our life is to be and that our life is to be shaped by God's love for us.

Every human life has its shape. Everybody considers some things important and other things of less weight. Some people shape their lives by the pursuit of success or approval or comfort or knowledge, giving all their energy to such ends while other considerations fall by the wayside. Some people choose to let their lives be shaped by chance, by what happens to them day by day. For the Christian believer, the shape of life is the life of the Lord Jesus.

This suggests that faith is not some sort of formless good feeling. If we are to give ourselves to the real Christ, we must accept Christ as he really is: the Son of God who became a real human being, who reveals to us his heavenly Father's love, who died and rose from the dead, who sends us the Spirit, who saves us from our sinfulness, who gives us the Church to continue his own mission. We must accept Christ and shape ourselves in conformity with him. There is a definite content to faith.

It is possible, of course, to oversimplify faith by identifying it purely and simply with its content, as if faith were a matter of accepting a certain number of truths rather than accepting the love and the life of a real person. Faith implies commitment as well as content. But the fact remains that, just as belief without commitment to the person of Jesus remains an intellectual exercise, so also commitment without content remains an exercise in emotionalism.

Faith is a source of ultimate security for the believer. The believer knows that God's love in our lives cannot be overcome by anything except our own rejection of it. At the same time, faith includes a sense of risk. It is not that the Lord around whom we shape our lives is not worthy of trust, but rather that our relationship with him may lead us into strange and even frightening paths. Our focus on the life of Christ in us may sometimes demand things of us that we didn't expect. It may call for efforts of which we do not think we are capable or lay on us burdens which seem too heavy to bear. This does not mean that our faith is misplaced, but rather that God's love is greater than our understanding and that, in making Christ the shape of our life, we ourselves are no longer the central character and controlling agent in it.

It is not for nothing that the two great examples of faith in the Old Testament, Abraham and Moses, were both called to leave the lands they knew and go on long journeys. There is a component of journeying for each of us in faith. We ourselves change as life develops. None of our relationships ever stays the same. We relate to our parents differently at 35 than we did at 15. We relate to God differently, too. At one time we may look on God as a kind of cosmic Santa Claus who spends all his time making toys for us to play with. At another stage we may look on God as lawgiver and judge. At still another we may come to know God as a friend who knows us better than we know ourselves and who loves us in ways that go far beyond our understanding. Some people come to know God as a burning personal presence who enlightens and transforms their spirit to the point of ecstasy.

People often experience confusion and frustration as they pass from one stage of faith to another because they are not sure what is happening to them. But it is not God or God's love which is changing, but we who receive and respond to it. We deal with the same faith and the same reality, the same relationship, but a relationship that evolves as we ourselves change.

It is also possible to lose faith. This is not a change in the quality of the relationship, but a total breaking off. People can become so interested in the secondary features of their lives that they lose sight of its main focus. Sometimes they decide that living in the Lord is simply too painful or too difficult to continue. Faith is a gift, a gift that can be lost through inattention as well as by deliberate decision.

What does all this mean in practice? What should we do to foster the faith that is in us and help it to develop? For one thing, we must let the Lord be alive in us. We must look on him not as a historical character from the past or as a far-off abstraction, but as living at the center of our lives. We must try to get to know him better from his teaching in sacred Scripture and through the Church.

We must also be conscious that our life as a believer has a definite shape, a focus that welcomes some things and necessarily excludes others. We have to keep that shape before our consciousness and keep trying to understand how the circumstances of our life fit into it. How do work and recreation and friendships contribute to the shaping of our life into the form of Christ? Are the problems and challenges we face the result of our own narrowness or are they somehow stages on our lifetime journey with Christ? Are there elements in our life that simply don't belong there if we are trying to shape it to the form of the Lord Jesus?

Above all, we must treasure our faith. We must nourish it in prayer and reflection. We must guard it from the meaningless distractions which would undermine it. We dare not take it for granted because faith is not just an interesting sidelight to our existence, but its very center. Our acceptance of God's love in Christ is what gives meaning and purpose to our life. Without faith there is no living in the Lord. Without faith there is not much real living at all.

For Discussion

1) What can you do to foster the development of faith in your life?

2) Do you know any people who seem to have lost their faith? How or why does this happen?

3) Is the quality of your faith now the same as it was five or ten years ago?

Hope: The Direction

If faith is the fundamental virtue that gives focus and form to our life, hope is the fundamental virtue that gives it direction.

In our everyday life, hope directs much of what we do. It draws us from one thing to another. The undergraduate studies hard at college to become a doctor someday. The person in business invests energy in work in the hope of making a profit. Hope directs us from where we are to where we want to be. Hope has to do with an "already," a situation in which we see possibilities, and with a "not yet," a fulfillment that is still to come. If there were no connection between the "already" and the "not yet," there would be no reason to strive to move from the one to the other. Hope is that connection.

It is the same with living in the Lord. Our heavenly Father has given us an "already": the life of Christ as our life, the promise of eternal happiness with God. But we find ourselves in the "not yet." Our lives are filled with limitation and frustration. We are infected with sinfulness. It is clear that we have not yet arrived at what God has promised us. Is there any reason to expect that we ever will? There is. And the reason is hope, the gift of confidence that God's promises are not in vain. Hope is the linkage between the "already" and the "not yet" as we live in the Lord.

The New Testament speaks about hope often. St. Paul tells the Romans, "Therefore, since we have been justified by faith, we have peace with God through our Lord Jesus Christ, through whom we have gained access [by faith] to this grace in which we stand, and we boast in hope of the glory of God. Not only that, but we even boast of our afflictions, knowing that affliction produces endurance, and endurance proven character, and proven character, hope..." (Romans 5:1-4). Later in the same letter he says, "For in hope we were saved. Now hope that sees for itself is not hope. For who hopes for what one sees? But if we hope for what we do not see, we wait with endurance" (Romans 8:24-25).

The First Letter of Peter tells its readers to "sanctify Christ as Lord in your hearts. Always be ready to give an explanation to anyone who asks you for a reason for your hope..." (1 Peter 3:15).

From these Scripture texts it is clear that hope is one of the characteristic qualities of the Christian believer. In fact, hope is the fundamental gift that Christianity offers the world.

It is easy to see the importance of hope if we look at human life without it. This is not a merely academic exercise, since one of the most pervasive spiritual maladies of our time is radical hopelessness, a state of having nothing significant to look forward to.

We all want to know, "What can I look for from my life? Is what I have all there is?" Unless there is some ultimate hope, there are only two possible answers to those questions. On one extreme is presumption: the acceptance of what is at hand as a personal achievement and as final, with nothing more to come. If we are moderately successful and comfortable and happy in our lives, we settle for that. We look for no further fulfillment because we have already managed, on our own, to get all there is. The other extreme is despair: to look on what we do not have, on all the potential that will remain unrealized, on all the sufferings that lie around us or ahead of us, and conclude that this must be the way it was meant to be. Failure is all there is.

Where does one go from either of those positions? The only logical next step is simply to turn away from life either when the superficial fulfillment which we think we have achieved for ourselves begins to disintegrate or when the pain of desperation becomes too heavy to bear. Albert Camus, an influential modern philosopher, has said that the only real question in human existence is the question of suicide. If there is no hope, he was right.

For the Christian believer things are different. Belief doesn't necessarily make life any easier. The believer is always confronted with the meaning of success and failure, and ultimately with the question of death. But hope gives the believer's life a special dimension. For the believer there is Another at work in life, Another who gives life meaning now and who promises an ultimate and final fulfillment beyond superficial (and ultimately unsatisfying) achievements, beyond the limitations and wounds of earthly existence. The Lord Jesus, whose life we share, died even as we shall die, but death was not the end for him. Death is not the end for us, either, because God has given us the hope that we will pass beyond death into a new and glorious existence, as Jesus did.

The test for presumption or despair or hope is death. In the face of death we ask ourselves, "Is this all there is?" The person without hope must answer, "Yes." The person gifted with Christian hope will answer, "No. Not by a long shot."

Is the Christian believer, then, necessarily an optimist? Emphatically so, if we look at ultimates. Hope enables the believer to look forward to every next step in life with courage and trust, because the believer knows that, when all is said and done, the story of his or her life is going to have a happy ending. Hope enables the believer to keep moving with confidence, because we always have someplace still to go until we reach the final fulfillment that God has promised us. It is hard to see how the believer can be anything but an optimist, one who always looks forward to the best.

This is not to suggest that the person of hope is satisfied with everything the way it is or does not see the suffering and cruelty and injustice that is part of the world around us. Those things are real. Any thinking person knows that we cannot make evil go away by pretending that it isn't there; no thinking person holds that we are allowed to sit back and simply wait for things to get better. Things may very well get worse. We are called to effort, to do all we can to care for ourselves, to heal suffering, to oppose cruelty, to overcome injustice. But as persons of hope, we know that such a struggle is not without purpose, and that, in the end, God will win out. Christian believers must be long-term optimists, but that does not mean that they must disregard what exists here and now.

How do we live out this gift of hope in practice?

For one thing, we must be careful not to settle too comfortably into the world and into our lives. We have to keep reminding ourselves that we still have something to do and someplace to go beyond the here and now, and that we cannot make it on our own. The society in which we live probably provides more comfort and distraction than any other in the history of humanity. If we choose, we can keep ourselves fully occupied with food and drink, with amusement, information and achievement. If we do, we run the risk of forgetting that the "already" is not the "not yet" and that the "not yet" is beyond our own achievement. Consumerism can easily lull us into accepting the idea that what we have or what we can get is all there is. If we want to stay strong in Christian hope, we ought to be a little suspicious of the world around us and a little uncomfortable in what is only a temporary dwelling.

On the other side of the practice of hope is the question of worry. It might be interesting to do an inventory of what we worry about in our lives. Is it all temporary stuff, questions of interest only here and now? Do we tend to identify present problems with ultimate threats? Jesus spoke to his followers about the lilies of the field and the birds of the air (see Matthew 6:25-34). His point was not that we shouldn't make reasonable provision for ourselves, but that there is more to our destiny than food and clothes. Concern about mundane matters should not preclude attention to our final destiny.

Comfort can make us presumptuous and worry can lead us to despair. Both are incompatible with hope. Neither is appropriate for those who have undertaken the challenge of living in the Lord.

For Discussion

1) What makes you comfortable in your life? What makes you uneasy?

2) What are your hopes for tomorrow? For next year? For the end of your life?

3) What evidence do you have that God is reliable?

Love: The Motion

Faith gives the basic focus to a believer's life and hope gives it direction. Love gives it motion and activity.

If we wished to list all the passages of the Bible that deal with love in any way, we would have to reproduce the whole volume because, in one way or another, all Scripture is concerned with love and with the relationships in which love is expressed.

In the New Testament we read about the Father's love for Jesus ("This is my beloved Son, with whom I am well pleased" [Matthew 3:17b]) and for us ("...God so loved the world that he gave his only Son..." [John 3:16a]), about Jesus' love for the Father ("...[T]he world must know that I love the Father" [John 14:31a]) and for us ("As the Father loves me, so I also love you. Remain in my love" [John 15:9]).

We read about our love for God ("We know that all things work for good for those who love God..." [Romans 8:28a]), our love for Jesus ("If you love me, you will keep my commandments" [John 14:15]) and our love for each another ("...[L]ove one another. As I have loved you, so you also should love one another" [John 13:34b]).

Jesus tells us that the central commandment is a commandment to love ("You shall love the Lord, your God, with all your heart...and your neighbor as yourself" [Luke 10:27b, d]) and St. Paul says that, whatever gifts and qualities we may have, we are nothing at all without love (see 1 Corinthians 13:1-3).

19

We all have a kind of instinctive grasp of love. Two friends see in each other something to admire, qualities that attract attention and response. The attraction invites the friends to share their gifts with one another, each offering to the other what he or she has in order to draw nearer to the good in the other. They spend time together; they go places together; they share their deepest thoughts with each other. All of this takes place not so that one can get possession of the other and use up the other for personal enjoyment, like a piece of candy, but simply in order to share the benefit of the good that is in the other. Love is the giving of ourselves to the goodness of somebody else just because of who and what that somebody is.

Real love, therefore, is generous, not self-serving. It is both accepting and respectful. It is a two-way process. It is concerned not with getting some specific benefit, but with the giving of ourselves. If we had to venture a definition, we might say that love is radical self-sharing.

Now let's consider the love between God and ourselves, that basic quality that constitutes one of the foundations of living in the Lord. (Later we will deal with other kinds of love.)

In a way, God's love for us doesn't make any sense. God is already totally fulfilled in the love that exists between Father, Son and Holy Spirit. God doesn't need anything or anyone else in order to be happy. Yet God loved us anyway and, in loving us, God causes us to be. The fact that we are here is a sign that God wants us, respects us, is interested in us—that God loves us. There's no explaining that. It's just the way things are. At the root of everything that exists lies the mystery of God's free, unsolicited, creative love.

But there is still more. In order to make this love clearer and more accessible to us, God became part of the created world. Knowing how hard it is for us even to imagine what God is and how much God loves us, God came to us as one of our own. In Jesus we see God living and acting in human terms, teaching, healing, expending his life for our benefit so that we can grasp that the glory of both God and humankind lies in self-giving, in selfless love.

God invites us to respond to all this in the same way: God calls us to love.

Loving God implies several things. For one, we must know God as God really is. If we look on God merely as lawgiver and punisher of wrong, our response will be fear rather than love. If we look on God as a kind of philosophical principle, totally detached from our world, our response may be admiration, but it will not be love. But if we know and accept God as loving creator and generous redeemer, as calling us to share the divine happiness—as lovable—then we can love God. Loving God presumes faith.

Likewise, we have to know ourselves as we really are. We have to be aware that we are precious to God, that we are worth something to God in spite of our limitations and our sinfulness. If all we see in ourselves is shame and failure, there is no point in giving ourselves to God in love because there would be no point in God's being concerned about us. Love of God includes an appropriate respect for ourselves.

We also have to be aware that God doesn't need our love and doesn't get anything out of it. Our love does God no favor. *We* are enriched and enlivened by our love for God. When God invites our love, it is for the sake of our own good, not God's. The call to love God is one of God's basic gifts to us.

It is for this reason that loving God is also closely connected with love for our neighbor. God isn't in need, but our neighbor is. All we can "do for" God in love is to do what we can for the well-being of others whom God loves.

Finally, love is an exercise of our will. It involves wanting and doing, not just feeling good about somebody else. What, then, are we to want and do in loving God? Put most simply, we are to make ourselves like the one we love. We are to make ourselves— or allow God to make us—godly. This includes a deep sense of reverence and submission. It includes sharing God's gifts with those around us. It includes collaborating in the development of the world God has given us for our use. Obviously it means rooting out of our lives whatever keeps us apart from God. Loving God means deliberately and consciously living in the Lord.

At a more immediate level, the most fundamental element in loving God is a deep and personal knowledge and friendship with Christ Jesus. In Jesus the Father gives us himself. It is in Jesus that we respond. We are called to acknowledge the presence of Jesus in our hearts. We must be familiar with him, comfortable in his presence, willing to share with him our thoughts and words and actions. Jesus is real and he is here. We have to keep ourselves aware of that and respond accordingly.

We also foster our love for God by looking for him in every corner of our life, not just in the depth of our hearts. The sunrise and the rain are reflections of God. So are the gifts and talents of our friends. So are the words of the poets and the paintings of the artists. The fact that there are millions of species of plants and animals says something about God and God's love. If love for God is going to be the center of our life, then we must be attentive to God wherever we can find God. And we can find God everywhere if we develop the habit of simply being attentive.

But all this is only the beginning. We will only be able fully to understand what loving God means when we have worked at it for a lifetime and come to experience its final significance in the light of God's own presence in heaven.

Faith, hope and love constitute our basic orientation to God. They are the fundamental qualities of God's self-communication with us and of our response. And each of them is necessary for our being in God. If we have no basic form and focus in faith, we have nothing to hope for and no reason for loving. If we have the direction of hope but not the motion and action of love, we remain stationary. And love without focus or direction is simply meaningless.

But in the final analysis, it is love that matters most. Love for God in the context of faith and hope constitutes living in the Lord.

For Discussion

1) How have you experienced love in your life? Is God involved?

2) What difference would it make if there were no love for God in your life?

3) Why is intimacy an element of love?

Friendship: Responding to Our Neighbor's Goodness

Friendship can mean many things, from superficial acquaintance to a lifetime of intimacy and sharing. Some friendships we have to work at; others just seem to happen. Marriage is a kind of friendship, too. Friendship is really what loving our neighbor is all about.

God's word in Scripture speaks often about friendship, the loving relationship of human beings. At the very beginning God said, "It is not good for the man to be alone. I will make a suitable partner for him" (Genesis 2:18b, c). In the life and teaching of Jesus, friendship holds a prominent place. "No one has greater love than this, to lay down one's life for one's friends" (John 15:13). Besides his circle of close followers, Jesus seems to have had lots of other friends as well. There were Martha and Mary and Lazarus, plus a whole troop of less savory people, so that Jesus' enemies looked down on him for being "a friend of tax collectors and sinners" (Luke 7:34b). Jesus was a friendly man.

What, then, is friendship? And what has it to do with love of neighbor? Friendship is born when we see good in somebody else and want to share that good, offering in return the good that is in us. The good we see in the other may be expressed in a pleasant personality or intelligence or creativity or any of a thousand other qualities. We find it attractive and want to bask in its light, not because of what we get out of it, but simply because it is lovable. Loving our neighbor means responding to our neighbor's goodness.

Ultimately, every friendship involves the goodness of God. We are all the result of God's lavish love for us. Everything we find admirable in others or in ourselves is somehow a reflection of the goodness of God, a piece of God's greatness, as it were, apportioned to a creature. This is why friendship is an important feature of living in the Lord.

We need to love others because none of us is complete in ourselves. Each of us has a special set of gifts and talents, but none of us has everything. In reaching out in love to others, we somehow contribute to our own fulfillment. In reaching out in love to others, we are also reaching out to the ultimate richness and completion of God.

People without friends, unloving and unloved, suffer from a radical disability that not only keeps them from being in touch with others but also from being fully themselves. The person without friends is simply not what God meant a human being to be. The stock example of such a person is Scrooge in Dickens' *A Christmas Carol*. Scrooge doesn't love anybody and won't let anybody love him. As a result he faces an ultimate isolation that is really an image of hell.

Lots of elements go into loving our neighbor. It involves self-disclosure and respect for the other. It carries with it a certain vulnerability: In reaching out to our neighbor we enable the neighbor to hurt us. All love is a kind of self-sharing; to a certain extent, every friendship carries with it a giving up of self for the good of the friend. Sometimes friendship is difficult, because drawing close to another and allowing another to draw close can require considerable effort. Sometimes friendship calls for forgiveness, for willingness to love the friend in spite of the harm that he or she may have done to us.

At the same time, loving another is a unifying experience. It carries us out of ourselves to become one with another. It breaks down barriers and widens the horizons of the world for all those who share in it. In the process of loving, our capacity to love increases and the circle of those we love and who love us becomes wider.

In all this, the true model of friendship (as well as the goal of friendship) is the Lord Jesus, whose life constitutes the core of our living, whose presence motivates our doing, whose example of selfless giving is the model on which we are called to base our lives. He is the friend par excellence, and in his friendship for us he teaches us how to be friends with others. We are called to be human as God is human in Jesus. And Jesus laid down his life for his friends.

We can understand friendship better if we look at its opposites.

The opposite of love is hatred. If love and friendship consist in seeing and treasuring the good that is in other people, hatred consists in the denial of such good. When we say that somebody is just "no good," we are saying that there is nothing to love in that person, and that therefore it is appropriate to write off or reject or even do harm to that person. But if we are aware of the universal love of our heavenly Father, if we recall that a person's very existence is a sign of God's care and respect for that person, if we remind ourselves that the Lord Jesus became human in order to assert the worth of all men and women, then it becomes clear that hating anybody for any reason is simply wrong. We have no right to be hostile to anyone whom God loves.

When Jesus tells us that we must love our enemies and do good to those who hate us (see Luke 6:27), he is not saying that we should feel an emotional attachment to those who do evil to us. He is saying that we must respect the good that God has put in them and be willing to foster and cultivate it. What we are to love in those who hate us is not their hatred but the essential good that is in everyone simply because they are creatures of a loving God. In telling us to love our enemies, Jesus is telling us that one who lives in the Lord should not have any enemies, only friends.

Hatred is less harmful to the one we hate than it is to us. In rejecting somebody we are cutting ourselves off from them and to that extent cutting ourselves off from a unique manifestation of the Lord. We are deliberately refusing the gifts God offers us in the other.

The other opposite of friendship is selfishness or possessiveness. Real love for our neighbor includes reverence, respecting our neighbor for what he or she is. When our friendship is possessive, we associate with others only to the extent that they are immediately useful or comforting to us. When others stop being "fun," we drop them. In the extreme form, we try to control another so that his or her whole worth depends on the benefit it can confer on us. We try to make one whose dignity rests on a relationship with God into our own psychological slave. That's not much better than hatred.

Friendship, our love for our neighbor, is not something we should take for granted in our lives. It's something we need to treasure and it's something we need to work at. We should consciously appreciate our friends. Sometimes it's helpful to try to understand what makes each of them so special to us, what it is that attracts us to them. When we review our friendships we are really examining the ways in which God reveals the divine likeness to us in other human creatures.

We should search for new and better ways to respond to the blessings that come to us through others. No human relationship can remain static for very long. As we grow to understand others and ourselves better, our relationships should deepen and mature. They should become more understanding, more generous, more unselfish. The lesson of Jesus' life is that human existence has value only in what we give away to those we love.

And we should rejoice in our human relationships. God has made us such that we cannot live alone. It is only in loving relationships that we really become ourselves. It is only in living for others that we are really living in the Lord.

For Discussion

1) Who are your friends? Why?

2) How have you experienced difficulty in friendship?

3) Is there any difference between "friends" and "neighbors"?

Family:
Primary Learning Place

People find many reasons for pessimism about the family these days: Men and women live together without any commitment to one another. Unborn children are killed by abortion. Working parents must hire outsiders to look after their children. Divorce is rampant. Young people are faced with temptations to sexual activity and drug use that were simply unknown a few decades ago. The kind of family that many of us remember—a father who provided the income, a mother who looked after the home and the children, close-knit brothers and sisters—seems the exception. We wonder where it's all going to end.

It might be well to recall two things: The first is that there have always been threats to families. In the "good old days" more babies died. Health care was frequently inaccessible for those who survived infancy. Life expectancy was shorter, and widows and orphans were often unprovided for. Retirement benefits were slim, if there were any. One great depression and several wars added to the burdens that families already bore. Things have been bad for families before now.

The second thing that we ought to remember is that the family, no matter how threatened it may seem, is still the means God uses to bring human beings into existence and to prepare them for mature participation in the world. Families are still the context in which most people meet Christ for the first time and come into contact with his Church. Pope John Paul II has reminded us that the future of the world and of the Church passes through the family. So as long as God is interested in the future of the world and of the Church, God will not—cannot—be absent from family life.

God has always worked in and through and for the family unit. The chosen people of the Old Testament saw themselves as one family, all descended from Abraham. When the time came for God to enter human history in Jesus, we hear about his family, about Mary and her husband Joseph, about her cousin Elizabeth. Later, in Jesus' public life, people identify him through his family: "Is this not Jesus, the son of Joseph? Do we not know his father and mother?" (John 6:42 a, b).

In the inspired writings of St. Paul to the young Churches, we find several important messages that deal with the implications of family life for living in the Lord: Wives and husbands should show reverence and love for one another; children should obey their parents; parents should treat their children with gentleness (see 1 Corinthians 7:1-7; Ephesians 5:21—6:4).

The concern for family life that God and the Church have shown over the ages is not just due to the way new life is generated or the many years of care infants need before they can survive on their own. Equally important to God and the Church is the consciousness of what it means to be a human being and what it means to be alive in the Lord, an awareness that generally comes through the family.

One of the most fascinating features of being human is the wide range of possibilities we enjoy. We can be dull or creative, gentle or cruel, understanding and generous or self-centered and narrow. We are born with a unique combination of talents and gifts which will develop into our own special personality in the years ahead. But the way that we develop, the balance among the various components of our personality, depends to a great extent on what we see and hear and experience from the people around us, especially those who are closest to us: our family.

The family is the primary learning place. Our parents and grandparents, our brothers and sisters, our aunts and uncles and cousins are all our teachers in one way or another. And the lessons we learn from them are the most fundamental lessons of all. In the family we are taught to choose from a great menu of human possibilities and values, a menu that includes such items as love and trust as well as success, money, power, position, comfort. In the family we learn about fatherhood and motherhood and friendship, fundamental concepts that influence the way we relate to other people throughout our life and even the way we relate to God. In the family we learn about Jesus and the Church, about prayer and basic spirituality. We learn about freedom and responsibility. Sometimes we also learn about greed and anger and cruelty and drunkenness and infidelity. Whatever else may go on in the family, it is a place of learning.

And it is not just in our childhood and youth that we learn the lessons of faith and humanity from our family. In adulthood, children can continue to learn about trust and patience and wisdom as they watch their parents grow older. Nor is it just children who learn from their elders. Parents can learn about faith and hope and love from their children. They can come to a deeper realization of God's providence in human life as they watch their children grow up. Just as human development continues as long as we live on this earth, so does the enrichment which we are able to draw from our families.

This learning does not happen, of course, through formal lessons. Much of it does not happen through words. It happens through experience and observation, and a great deal of it is not even conscious. Whether we know it or not, whether we intend it or not, there is always teaching and learning going on in the family. We communicate most by what we are, and our deepest beliefs and our most personal values necessarily influence those with whom we share family life. God has made us all to be learners and teachers, whether we choose to be or not, and the learning and teaching takes place, to a great extent, in our families.

We shouldn't be surprised if the blessings of family life carry a price tag. Family life requires sacrifice. As the family goes about its task of teaching humanity, the wishes of one member sometimes conflict with the needs of another. We have to give way to each other. Sometimes, in order to be true to its own principles, a family will have to deny itself possessions and comforts that others enjoy.

Family life requires honesty. There isn't much point in trying to pretend we are something we are not in the context of the family, because we will not succeed. Our attempt to hide ourselves will only turn into a lesson in concealment. If we don't like what we are, if we suspect that we are not everything we should be or don't want our family members to be like us, it is much healthier to try to change and develop ourselves than to pretend we are something we are not.

Family life requires attention. Although much of what goes on in the learning place of the family happens unconsciously, it does not happen by chance. We need to reflect on how things are going in our family, on what is being taught and what is being learned, on what we are really saying to one another. Sometimes we simply need to spend time together, lest we find ourselves communicating that everything else is more important than our family. We also need to test the values that our culture presents to us. Are these the values that we want our family to accept?

Most of all, family life requires the Lord Jesus. If the whole goal of human existence is living in the Lord, then the Lord has to be an acknowledged part of all our teaching and learning and development. This suggests regular and unembarrassed prayer in the family. It suggests articulate faith in Christ and reverence and loyalty toward his Church. It suggests accepting the Lord as a member of the family.

God reveals himself to us as Father. Jesus makes himself our brother. Living in the Lord, then, is really a family affair, and being a family calls for living in the Lord.

For Discussion

1) What are the most important things parents should exemplify for their children?

2) How is your family's life today different from that of your childhood? Is the difference good or not?

3) How are religious values communicated in your family?

Civil Society:
The Wider Context

There is no such thing as a totally private person or a totally private life. God made us to exist together. We come into being and learn about our humanity through our families. We grow and enrich ourselves and others by sharing our lives in different kinds of friendships. In both family and friendship we give and we receive. In both we carry out certain responsibilities.

A third level of the human community is that of civil society: our neighborhood, our town, our country, our world. We cannot be inattentive to civil society any more than we can be inattentive to family and friends if we would live in the Lord.

Jesus himself tells us that civil society has a claim on us. When his enemies were trying to trick him into taking a position either as a revolutionary or a collaborationist by asking whether they should pay taxes, he answered, "...[R]epay to Caesar what belongs to Caesar and to God what belongs to God" (Matthew 22:21). In this saying, Jesus indicates that civil society, while it is not the be-all and end-all of our human existence, does make demands on us to which we must respond.

Involvement in civil society has always been part of the Christian vocation. We have no more choice about being in civil society than we have about being in a family. Both are necessary for our existence as human beings. Without civil society there would be no laws to defend us, no services to provide for our needs, no means of redress to help us deal with the inevitable disputes that arise whenever human beings are together. The only alternative to civil society is savagery, and God did not create us to be savages.

Sometimes we are inclined to look on civil society as a given, as an establishment for which we bear no personal responsibility. We see how complicated modern government is, how many problems it must face, and we tell ourselves that we have to accept it as it is because there is nothing much that individuals like ourselves can do to make it better or to correct its shortcomings.

In fact, although civil society is part of God's plan for us human creatures, its concrete form is the result of human decisions. Any society is what it is because people have made it that way. A society is capitalistic or socialistic because at some point men and women decided that it should be so. A country is inclined to look out for the rich rather than the poor or to provide educational and economic opportunities for the many rather than the few because, at some point, laws were made by human lawmakers to bring about such a condition.

But conditions created by human decisions can be changed by human decision. The way civil society works today may be the result of yesterday's decisions, but the way it works in the near or distant tomorrow is the result of decisions that are being made—or avoided—by people like us today. We cannot simply accept civil society as a given because it is we who create it.

Given the complexity of the society in which we live, it is clear that few of us are going to have much influence on it as individuals. But society is not something that comes about because of one person alone. It is always the result of collaboration, of women and men working together to make things the way they want them to be. We are powerless only when we stand alone.

And where is the Lord Jesus in all this? We know that he wants his sisters and brothers to live together in justice and peace. Because civil society is humanity's main instrument for justice and peace, the Lord's will applies there. We also know that the Lord Jesus generally works through human beings, through the minds and wills of persons like us. Consequently, if Jesus' loving will for the world is going to be carried out, it will be through the cooperation of those who live in him and through their determination to make society what he wants it to be.

Two observations need to be made in this context: First, we U.S. Catholics have a special responsibility to society in these times. We have come a long way from our immigrant origins. Over the past several decades we have become one of the best educated and the most affluent religious groups in the country. This position carries responsibility with it. Because of what we have achieved or been given, we are called to make our voices heard in the development of our nation and our world. It is not a matter of forcing everybody to become Catholic or of imposing our religious beliefs on others. Rather, because of the resources at our disposal, we have a responsibility to take a serious, consistent and thoughtful role in the process that molds civil society.

Secondly, we are called to give special attention to the powerless and the poor. These are the members of our society who are least able to look out for themselves and who need the voice and support of those who, like us, are in a better position to be heard. We owe that kind of concern to the poor simply because Christ loves them as he loves us. They are our brothers and sisters because we all form one family in him.

How does all this translate into practice?

We must consciously accept our responsibility for civil society as part of our vocation to live in the Lord. Taking responsibility for society is not just a nice hobby for those who find that sort of thing interesting. It is part of what God calls us to as sharers in divine life and as agents of God's love for the men and women around us. Social concern is as much a part of our faith as are prayer and Sunday Mass, and we must deliberately accept it as such.

Further, we should inform ourselves about the issues that face our civil society. It is true that the major issues are very complex and that persons of goodwill can differ on how to address them. But, if we are to take seriously our responsibility for civil society, we have to know what the issues are and we have to know something about them. In our time these issues include such questions as abortion, arms control and disarmament, racial justice, government policies affecting family life, food and agriculture, health, housing, poverty, unemployment, drugs and ecology. These matters are not just the concerns of public servants. They are our concerns because they are the Lord's concerns. They have a claim on our personal spirituality.

At very least, we must conscientiously exercise our right to vote. Conscientious voting involves much more than just showing up on election day and casting a ballot. We need to know what the candidates are saying about the issues and how serious they are about them. If a candidate is already in office, how does his or her record conform with earlier campaign promises? Are the candidate's stands on the various issues consistent? Will the candidate or the party be in a position to carry promises? Our task as voters is to discern which issues are more important and which less, and whether the candidates put the same relative importance on these issues as we do.

Living in the Lord includes a wider context than "me and Jesus." Living in the Lord takes place wherever human interests are at stake and wherever human decisions are made.

For Discussion

1) What would you like to change in your city or in the country? Why? How?

2) What issues do you think you need to know more about in order to exercise responsible citizenship?

3) How does your Catholic faith influence your life in civil society?

Work:
Obligation and Opportunity

Sometimes work seems to be a duty, a heavy obligation that we must fulfill as part of our human destiny. At other times work seems to be an opportunity, a chance to do something that is going to make a difference to ourselves and to those around us. Whatever else it may be, work is a constant part of our life. When the age for retirement comes, we approach it with mixed feelings—glad, in a way, that we won't have to work anymore yet apprehensive that our life will be less meaningful.

Jesus was identified by his early hearers as a blue-collar worker: "Is he not the carpenter, the son of Mary...?" (Mark 6:3a). He speaks of his mission as work in collaboration with his Father: "My Father is at work until now, so I am at work" (John 5:17b). Many of his parables are about workers: shepherds, housewives, farmers, servants, fishermen, merchants. Workers obviously meant something to Jesus.

St. Paul reminds the Corinthians how he has exercised his ministry: "in toil and hardship, through many sleepless nights, through hunger and thirst, through frequent fastings, through cold and exposure" (2 Corinthians 11:27). The Thessalonians, expecting Christ's imminent return, had some strange ideas about work that Paul felt compelled to correct: "...[A]spire to live a tranquil life, to mind your own affairs, and to work with your

[own] hands, as we instructed you, that you may conduct yourselves properly toward outsiders and not depend on anyone" (1 Thessalonians 4:11-12). "In fact, when we were with you, we instructed you that if anyone was unwilling to work, neither should that one eat" (2 Thessalonians 3:10).

Work can be very demanding, requiring energy and attention, consistency and patience. We have to work even when we don't feel like it. Often we don't see the results we wish; sometimes we feel unfairly treated. Yet we know that the only practical alternative to work is economic deprivation and misery.

But there is another side to work, perhaps the most important side: Work is more than a necessary evil or an obligation. It is also an opportunity to share in God's own creativity. Work is an important part of the spirituality of those who strive to live in the Lord.

God didn't finish the world in every last detail at creation. Some things God left to develop according to evolutionary laws. Other things God left to the energy and imagination of the chief creature in the world, the human creature.

To this human creature God gave the capacity and the challenge to take what had been created and carry it further, to share in God's concern for the world and for the human creature, to be a partner with God in the care that God has for the world.

Moreover, God entered the world as a human participant in Christ and called the followers of Christ to continue his life and his mission in the world. The imprint that these women and men leave on the world is no longer just their own human imprint, but the imprint of Christ himself. We are called to bring Christ to the world, the world that already exists and the world still coming to be. One basic way we respond to that calling is through work.

Every kind of decent human work is a contribution to God's creativity in Christ. The work a mother and father do to raise their children is participation in God's providence. So is the work of teachers who, in their fields of expertise, bring their students to greater knowledge and appreciation of God's works. Plumbers and carpenters make materials God has provided serve the greater comfort and health of human creatures. Salespersons and merchants assist in the distribution of the products of God's creativity and of human ingenuity. Factory workers use their skills in complicated collaborative efforts to produce goods for the well-being of others.

In the process of work, the worker produces something more than an object or a service. The worker also develops his or her own personal dignity. The results of the work are important, but these results are secondary to the human and spiritual enrichment that comes with working with the Lord in the process of creation. We work not just in order to *do* but also to *be*.

This is why the Church teaches that we may never look on a worker as a commodity, as just one more element in production, to be acquired as cheaply as possible and to be discarded when he or she becomes nonproductive. Human dignity must be safeguarded, no matter what the work is. To defend this dignity that is an essential element of work, the Church teaches about the rights of workers, about just wages and humane working conditions, about the devastating human cost of unemployment. The Church also teaches about workers' responsibility toward their employers, about diligence and honesty. In dealing with these matters the Church is not interfering in areas unrelated to its mission. The Church is simply spelling out the implications of its own teaching about creation and about human participation in God's activity.

Perhaps the most important element in the spirituality of work is to keep ourselves conscious of how our work carries forward God's creativity and Christ's love for his sisters and brothers. We should try to be aware of how what we do makes a

45

difference to the world, to the people around us and, most of all, to the Lord.

It is easy to get bored with what we do, to look on it as a task that we have to carry out in order to survive. (Even archbishops sometimes find themselves doing one thing after another just because it is their job.) If that mentality lasts very long, we can all lose one of the most important perspectives in our lives in the Lord. We do not work just for pay or out of a sense of obligation. We are fellow workers with the Lord, and we have to keep reminding ourselves of that if our work is to be spiritually significant.

Because of the dignity of our calling as cocreators, it is right that we take an appropriate pride in our work. We do not work just in order to keep our employer happy or just to keep our job. We work as agents of Christ and so we try to do our work carefully and honestly. We collaborate with those who work around us. It is right to take joy and satisfaction in what we do. According to Genesis 1:1—2:4a, at the end of the work of original creation, God pronounced it good and rejoiced in the work. It is fitting that we do the same.

We must also be aware that it is possible to go to excess in working, to work in a manner that is not in keeping with the dignity of the task that God has given us.

One such excess is an unhealthy competitiveness. If our whole goal in what we do is to do more or better than someone else, we have lost sight of what our work is really all about. We are not called to work in order to demonstrate that we are better, but to give grateful witness that God is good.

Another excess is that of the workaholic. This is the person whose whole life is work, for whom there is nothing else but the job. Family, friends, leisure, prayer, reflection—all take second place to work. For the workaholic work has become an addiction, an escape from all else, a flight from the human values that work is intended to enhance. The workaholic does not see himself or herself as subordinate to God in the ongoing aspects of creation, but rather as a kind of independent agent without whose activity the world would somehow cease to be. The temptation of the workaholic is the same as the original temptation besetting Adam and Eve: to be as gods.

Clearly, God does not call us to work so that we can prove our worth to our Maker. God already appreciates our worth better than we do. Moreover, in every life there are times when we cannot work. God does not write us off at those times. Yet God calls most of us for most of our lives to contribute through work to God's creation. God's own Son experienced the demands of work. That's why, for us, work is part of living in the Lord.

For Discussion

1) What difference does your work make to the world?

2) What satisfactions and dissatisfactions do you find in your work? How are they connected with spirituality?

3) Do the demands of your job ever conflict with the demands of your life in the Lord?

Prayer: Personal Communication With God

Jesus prayed a lot during his life on earth. Luke especially shows him in prayer. Luke's Jesus prayed after his baptism by John (3:21). As his reputation grew, "...he would withdraw to deserted places to pray" (5:16). Before he chose his 12 apostles, "...he departed to the mountain to pray, and he spent the night in prayer to God" (6:12). The transfiguration took place as Jesus was praying on the mountain (see 9:28). The prayer of Jesus induced his disciples to ask him to teach them to pray (see 11:1). Jesus prayed in the garden before he was arrested (see 22:41-44). And he prayed as he died on the cross: "Father, into your hands I commend my spirit" (23:46b).

Jesus also taught about prayer. "...[A]ll that you ask for in prayer, believe that you will receive it and it shall be yours. When you stand to pray, forgive anyone against whom you have a grievance, so that your heavenly Father may in turn forgive you your transgressions" (Mk 11:24b-25). He taught his followers to pray continually and never to lose heart (see Lk 18:1), to pray for those who mistreat them (see Luke 6:8), to pray in time of trial (see Luke 22:40). And he gave them a prayer model, the Lord's Prayer.

If prayer was such an important element in the life and teaching of Jesus, it must also be important to us who strive to live in the Lord.

Prayer is deliberate and conscious personal communication between ourselves and God. Every loving relationship calls for a sharing of self by persons who love one another. Sometimes the sharing involves the exchange of information. Sometimes it is just a matter of spending time together. Sometimes we encourage and affirm the person we love. Sometimes it is necessary to ask for forgiveness. But there can be no love without some sort of personal communication.

It's the same with prayer. Prayer is spending time with God—Father, Son and Spirit—opening ourselves up to God and allowing God to come closer to us. Sometimes we ask for things from God. Sometimes we thank God. Sometimes we affirm God's greatness and sometimes we ask God's pardon. Our prayer may be expressed in words, in thoughts, in feelings, in reverent attentiveness to Christ within us. But however prayer is expressed, whatever its tenor, prayer is a matter of bringing our whole human existence before God—the good and the bad, our hopes and our fears, our needs and our achievements—and dumping it out before God, sorting it through and talking it over with God. Prayer is the basic way we let God into our lives. Prayer is the way we personalize our association with the Lord. Prayer is how we come to personal knowledge of the Lord.

There are three aspects of prayer that we need to be clear about.

The first is that prayer doesn't change God. We don't pray because we have to convince God to give us what we need or to persuade God to keep on loving us. God has promised to do all that already, and the presence of Christ in our hearts attests to God's seriousness about the promise. Prayer doesn't change God, but it changes us. It allows God to get to us and to transform us. When we pray we set ourselves before the Lord and allow God to go to work on us. We allow ourselves to be led closer to God one step at a time in accord with God's plan for what is best for us.

Second, when we say that prayer is communication with God, it doesn't mean that prayer is just our speaking to the Lord. Prayer is also listening. In fact, listening may be the most important part of our communication with God. This is not to say that if we pray correctly we will hear a heavenly voice telling us in detail what we should do or be. Listening to God in prayer is, rather, a matter of presenting to God the various aspects of our life and reflecting on them in the light of what God has told us about the divine love for us and God's expectations of us. As we pray over a period of time, it will become clear to us that some things in our life need to be changed or that some of the problems we face are not insoluble or that we need to be more consciously aware of how active God already is in what is going on in and around us. In fact, God is communicating with us all the time. Prayer is simply the way in which we allow that communication to get through to us.

The third aspect of prayer that we need to be clear about is that prayer requires a certain degree of effort. Prayer is, in part at least, a skill, something that requires practice and time. We have to work at it and stick with it, just as we must work at any other important facet of our lives. God is the principal partner in the dialogue of prayer, to be sure, but the relationship cannot move forward unless we are willing to do our part.

Each Christian believer has a unique personal experience of prayer because prayer is an expression of an individual relationship with God in Christ. Yet there are some practical suggestions about prayer that Christian spirituality offers to everybody.

One of the greatest helps to prayer is to have enough organization in life to make prayer possible. There is an almost limitless amount of "noise" in our lives, claims on our attention that include the banalities of radio and TV, our daily contacts with the people around us and our own chattering stream of consciousness. God is indeed somewhere in the noise, but we also need times of deliberate quiet and attentiveness so that we can address God seriously and hear God clearly.

We have to set aside times in our daily routine to be with God. They don't have to be long periods, but they do have to be regular. Maybe it will be the time we spend going to work or coming home. Maybe it will be a few moments after the children have gone off to school. Perhaps we can pray as we take care of some of the tasks in our day that we do more or less automatically. Just sitting quietly in the evening and spending a few minutes with the Lord might be a better use of our time than watching one more TV program. Our relationship with God is too important to be relegated to the chance moments that occur only occasionally when everything else is done.

What should we pray about? About everything. A good way of praying is to take the various elements of our lives—family, work, problems, questions, fears—and bring them one by one into the presence of the Lord Jesus in our hearts. Because he lives in us, all these things are important to him just as they are to us. It is appropriate for us to share them with him, to pay attention to them in the light of his presence.

Scripture is another means of prayer. Scripture is God's word addressed to God's people. When we take a passage from the Bible, read it attentively, mull over it and open ourselves up to its meaning, we are listening to God. You don't have to be a professional Scripture scholar to use the Bible in prayer. After all, the word of God is not addressed just to Scripture scholars! There are many kinds of printed commentaries and audiotapes that can help deepen our appreciation of Scripture and to keep us from reading our own meaning into it. But God is speaking in Scripture—to us, here and now, today. If prayer is largely listening, there isn't anything better we could listen to.

In the Book of Revelation, the Spirit says to us, "Behold, I stand at the door and knock. If anyone hears my voice and opens the door, [then] I will enter his house and dine with him, and he with me" (3:20). The Lord offers to come into our house and be with us, side by side. Prayer is the handle on our side of the door.

For Discussion

1) When, where and how do you pray best?

2) What difference do you see between "prayers" and "prayer"?

3) What does it mean to you to pray for other people?

4) How would your life be different if you never prayed? If you prayed more?

Church:
Community of the Faithful

In a way, the whole New Testament is a book about the Church. In the Gospels we read about the life and the ministry of Jesus. When Jesus returned to his Father at the end of his earthly life, he assured his disciples that he would be with them still: "And behold, I am with you always, until the end of the age" (Matthew 28:20b).

The way Jesus stayed with his first followers and the way he stays with us is through the Church. The Church is the Body of Christ, St. Paul tells the Colossians: "He is the head of the body, the church" (1:18a). In Acts we read about the Church's first days, about the struggles to clarify the Church's relationship with Judaism and with the rest of the world. In the letters of St. Paul we meet the local Churches at Rome, Corinth and elsewhere as these small groups of people grow in their relationship with Christ and with one another. The last book of the New Testament, the Book of Revelation, is concerned with the Church, too; its context is the trials and persecutions that the Church was beginning to face. In almost the final words of the New Testament, the author of Revelation shows us Christ saying, "I, Jesus, sent my angel to give you this testimony for the churches" (22:16).

The Church was important to Jesus and to his first followers. It is important for us, too.

55

Without the Church there would be no Scripture, no sacraments, no liturgy, no encouragement and support from other believers, no clear and sure teaching about the meaning of Jesus' life and words, no specific context in which to look for Christ. Without the Church, Jesus would turn into a vague historical character, in danger of being remade into our own personal image. Without the Church there would be no Christian spirituality, because we would not have any realistic access to the One whose life we are called to live.

If the Church were exclusively the extension of the life and mission of Christ and nothing else, the Church would be much easier to deal with than it is. But things are not that simple. The Church is also the community of the faithful. This means that the Church includes not just Christ, but also ourselves. It includes good people and people who are not so good, people with whom we agree and people we find intolerable. The Church includes those whose love is an inspiration and comfort to us as well as those who have hurt us in the past and continue to hurt us now.

Because the Church is a community, it has laws and customs. There is authority in the Church, and wherever there is authority there are questions about its use. Sometimes those in authority seem to give the impression that they are the Church and that the others are merely there to obey. Sometimes the "others" assert their rights as sharers in the life of Christ to the extent that they reject even the rightful exercise of authority.

In order to resolve these tensions, people sometimes speak of the "institutional" Church as opposed to the "real" or "spiritual" Church, and take the position that the "institutional" Church isn't important, and that all we have to pay attention to is the "real" Church. In fact, but there is only one Church, the Church that is at one and the same time the extension of the presence and mission of Christ as well as the gathering of all of Christ's followers, the

Church that offers us the Scriptures and the sacraments as well as the structures and rules necessary in every human institution.

This means that the Church can be very messy at times. At its very heart there is the tension between divinity and humanity, between the all-embracing and constant love of Christ and the limited efforts of his followers to live up to what he offers us. In fact, the Church has always been messy. From its New Testament beginnings it has seen fights and misunderstandings as well as conspicuous holiness and heroism. It has shown the sinfulness and limitation of its human members, including its leaders, as well as the love and life of Christ, whose body it is. Being a member of the Church has never been easy simply because living in the Lord, as human individuals and human community, is never easy.

How are we to deal with all this richness and frustration as we make our spiritual journey in the Lord?

First of all, we must love the Church and treasure it. The easiest thing in the world is to zero in on the faults of priests and bishops and fellow believers and make them the center of our attention. Yet all this is only the surface of the Church, and not the complete surface at that. In the midst of all this is Christ, who loves us and who has made his Church one of the principal expressions of his love.

We should also try to take a comprehensive view of the Church. It is true that for most Catholic Christian believers, the parish is the ordinary means of contact with the Church. But the Church is bigger than our parish. The problems and the blessings that we experience in our parish are only a tiny part of a bigger picture that extends through the local Church (the diocese) to the Church universal and ultimately to the community of those who are united with Christ in heaven. If our view of the Church is too narrow, we run the risk of relating to a narrow Christ, an unreal Christ.

In addition, we need to remind ourselves occasionally that our life as members of the Church is not so much a matter of getting as of giving. Priests and sisters and professional lay ministers are not the only ones on whom the Church depends for its vitality. We all have a contribution to make, and that contribution is not just financial. We contribute to the life of the Church when we share our joys and sorrows in the community of the faithful, when we make available to other members our talents for service or compassion or organization. Sometimes we contribute to the life of the Church just by being part of it, by witnessing with our presence to our faith and hope and love. In all of this, it is not just we who are giving to the Church, but Christ who is enlivening his own body through us.

We also need to remind ourselves occasionally that our activity as members of the Church cannot limit itself to what goes on in parish or congregational life. The Church does not exist in order to be a Church, but to bring the Good News of Christ to the world at large, to family and neighborhood and work and civil society. The Church gathers us in to be with Christ, but the Church also sends us out to take Christ wherever we go. It is possible to be so involved with Church life that we lose sight of what the Church is really for. That can be as counterproductive as refusing to take part in the Church's life at all.

When all is said and done, Christian spirituality, living in the Lord, calls us to be active members of the real Church. The real Church includes our parish as well as the pope and Mother Teresa. The real Church has parish councils and finance committees as well as martyrs and missionaries. The real Church offers us the opportunity to be in close personal touch with the Lord Jesus as well as with his brothers and sisters—the good, the bad, the beautiful, the ugly. There is no point in searching for a community of believers without tension and challenge, because even if such a community exists, it is not the community of Christ.

We cannot get along without the Church because life and growth in the Lord are never just personal and private. The Lord offers us himself in the company of his brothers and sisters, our brothers and sisters. If we cannot find him there, we will never find him at all. If we try to dispense with the effort of being part of the community of believers, we are not really living in the Lord.

For Discussion

1) What do you think of first when you think of "Church"?

2) What is the most precious gift that the Church offers you? What do you have to offer to the Church?

3) What difference does the Church make in your everyday life?

Suffering:
Inescapable Mystery

There are as many kinds of suffering as there are sides to our human existence. In every dimension of our being we can feel pain, from the physical suffering of a broken bone or the flu to the mental anguish of ignorance or of knowing that we have done wrong. Sometimes we suffer from loneliness and sometimes we suffer from being with other people. We can suffer from what happens to us and we can suffer watching what is happening to someone we love. Sometimes whole nations are afflicted with common sufferings. In some lives, suffering seems rare; in others it is almost constant. But to a greater or less extent, suffering is part of every human life. No one is exempt from pain.

Jesus was familiar with suffering, too. He experienced fatigue and frustration, hunger and thirst. He knew that his mission would bring him into conflict with the authorities of his time and that it would end in pain and death: "...Jesus began to show his disciples that he must go to Jerusalem and suffer greatly from the elders, the chief priests, and the scribes, and be killed and on the third day be raised" (Matthew 16:21). And when the time came, he suffered degradation and abandonment as well as physical pain.

Jesus was also affected by the sufferings of others. He felt compassion for the blind and the lame and the deaf, for the bereaved and the poor. He felt sorry for the crowds when they were hungry. He reached out in pity to those who had wounded themselves by sin. Jesus was no stranger to suffering.

In the face of suffering, our own and that of others, we find ourselves asking questions. Why is this happening? What does it mean? Is life really supposed to be painful?

The Christian tradition speaks of suffering as a mystery. *Mystery* in this context means not only something we can't solve or understand, but also a situation or a series of events which involves a gradual revelation of God's presence and love. Thus we speak of the mysteries of Christ's life as well as of the mystery of suffering. We can't come up with a definitive explanation of suffering, but we know that God is somehow involved in it.

As we examine the mystery of suffering, some things are clear. Although God is involved in it, suffering does not for that reason become good. Nor is causing suffering virtuous. A loving Creator does not take pleasure in creatures' pain. Likewise, while some suffering comes to us as a result of our own wrongdoing, it is incorrect to assume that all suffering is a direct punishment for the sins of the sufferer. If that were the case, there would be no accounting for the sufferings of Jesus. Finally, suffering is not something that is visited on us for its own sake. It may be a by-product of other forces, it may be the occasion for God to show the divine love for us in mysterious ways, but it is never a goal in itself.

Often our suffering consists in coming up against human limitations. We contract diseases because the body is subject to weakness and infection. We can be hurt by other people's words because our understanding is limited by the boundaries of our own needs and experience. We suffer social injustice simply because society has not yet learned how to deal with all the forces at work in it. Even growth can be painful, as we move from a stage of our physical and mental development that has grown comfortable to another that seems threatening and difficult. Suffering is the price we pay for being imperfect, limited creatures in an imperfect, limited world. It is the product of our inborn vulnerability.

Some suffering *is* the result of sin. When we deliberately turn away from what God has made us to be or do, we inflict a kind of violence on ourselves which sooner or later involves pain. The sinfulness of others can bring us suffering, too, when we are the victims of their disordered behavior. Ultimately every sin brings suffering both to the sinner and to all others affected by the sin.

Somehow God is at work in all of this. If we take as our starting point the conviction that God loves us, that God is active in our lives, that God is all-powerful and God's ingenuity infinite, we begin to understand how God can turn even suffering to good purposes. Suffering is not the central reality. The Lord's love for us is. Everything else is secondary to that. Everything else is a means that God can use to draw us closer. If God can make the whole world out of nothing, God is also able to bring blessing out of pain.

Our life is a kind of tapestry that God weaves, using the various materials that are at hand, suffering included. If we look on one side, it seems to be a jumble of tangled threads. If we look on the other, we see the emergence of a pattern under the hand of the master craftsman. We easily see the jumble. God invites us—and helps us—to search for the pattern.

The worth or meaning of suffering does not depend so much on what the suffering is or where it comes from as on what God intends to bring out of it and the degree of acceptance we offer to God's planning. What does that mean in practice?

For one thing, we should not be surprised when suffering comes into our lives. To be sure, life is much more than suffering, but suffering is part of every life. Our culture tries to convince us that, if everything were as it could be, there would be no suffering, and that wherever there is suffering, it is there because somebody isn't doing his or her part. Some years ago an aspirin commercial spoke of a headache as "unfair." Marriages break up because people believe that any human association that requires effort and involves pain is unhealthy.

Because we are limited beings in a limited world, we simply cannot escape suffering. And if we try, we may find ourselves in a state of confusion and fear that is more painful than the suffering we seek to avoid. Christian spirituality consists of living in the real world with the Lord Jesus, and suffering is real.

Suffering calls for prayer. Our first reaction in suffering is to pray that it will go away. That's appropriate. But if the suffering does not go away, we must continue to pray nonetheless. This is a context in which the listening aspect of prayer is particularly important. God may not cause our suffering, and God may not approve of the way in which it comes to us, but God is involved in it nonetheless. We have to try to find God there, and that means we have to listen for God's voice in the midst of our pain. God will not shout at us. God will not give us all the answers to our suffering. But if we listen attentively in our prayer, we will be reassured, bit by bit, that God has not walked away from us and that there is more at issue here than pain.

In suffering we must pay particular attention to the Lord Jesus, who is in our hearts. Here is one who lived a human life like ours. Here is one acquainted with weakness, who experienced suffering. He understands us, loves us, is with us. Human relationships often grow deeper when the people involved in them have experienced adversity together. Our relationship with Christ will deepen as we take comfort in his suffering and share with him our own. Suffering together is an important part of living in the Lord.

For Discussion

1) How has suffering been a part of your life? Are you able to see God's work in any of it?

2) Why should you be concerned to alleviate the suffering of others?

3) What is the greatest suffering in our society? In our world? Can you do anything about it?

Aging: Burden or Gift?

Whatever our age, our life has elements of contentment and enthusiasm, but also elements of puzzlement and pain. We look forward to what is still to happen, yet we feel a degree of apprehension. We know that we really wouldn't want to be 39 years old forever, but we wonder what the 40th or 50th or 60th year will bring. Every new stage of our lives involves both moving on from what we have become and receiving new blessings and new challenges. Every advance in age is a loss; every advance in age is a gift. Every age brings the best years of our life. Every age moves us into a new chapter of our adventure. But constant throughout each period is our sharing in the love and the life of the Lord Jesus.

The final chapters of our life, the years we refer to as old age, are no different from the rest. Like all the others, old age involves opportunities and questions, joys and burdens.

The burdens of old age become ever clearer as we move into it. We don't seem to have as much energy as we did before; we tire more quickly. Our bodies seem to need more care and we become more concerned about our health and more careful about physical activity. We begin to suspect that our greatest accomplishments are behind us and that other people don't need us the way they used to. We may begin to fear that we will become a burden to our dear ones.

But there are also blessings in old age. One is that we are no longer required to achieve as we did before. We don't have to prove our worth by what we are able to do. Another blessing is that we don't have to continue to acquire. By the time they have grown old, most people find that their house is bigger than they can use, that they have more possessions than they want. It is time to give away rather than to seek for more. Children mature and are able to provide for themselves and so the responsibilities of parenthood lighten.

Older people also have the gift of time. Those who are younger tend to envy the opportunities that older people have to choose what they want to do, to engage in new activities, to be with their friends and loved ones for longer periods. Older people don't have to hurry so much.

Another gift of age is the gift of perspective. Thanks to the experience of a lifetime, older people are better able to see the difference between the important and the trivial, between tragedies and annoyances. They will have learned that no earthly burden lasts forever and that no earthly achievement is definitive. If they have been attentive to the Lord in their earlier years, they will have developed a sensitivity to God's presence in their lives and in the lives of those they love. This gift of perspective is what spiritual masters call wisdom.

But the greatest gift of old age may be the unique opportunity that older people have to master—and to share—a basic lesson that God wants to teach the human creatures God loves so much: the lesson of total dependence. It is true that God gives us talents and energies to do, to achieve, to earn, to be agents of Providence to others. But our real worth is not defined by our accomplishments, however great they may be. Our real worth arises from the attention God shows us. It is our dependence on God that makes us important.

This is easy to forget as we bustle about our life acquiring the skills we need to live in the world, reaching out to form relationships with other people, trying to make our contribution to civil society or the Church or the world of work. Unconsciously we strive to pay our own way wherever we go. If we are not careful, we begin to think that it is the Lord who needs us and that if we are no longer producing something or doing something the Lord will lose interest in us.

In giving us a period of life when we are able to do less and less for ourselves, God is calling us to remember that in the center of all of our activity has been not our own talents or abilities, but the life of the Lord Jesus which we have been given. When such a period comes, God reminds us—and reminds others through us—that everything we are and everything we have done is gift and that what is required of us is not the capacity to earn but the willingness to receive.

How, then, is an older person to practice living in the Lord? What is involved in the spirituality of old age?

We should look on old age not as an onus but as a gift, an opportunity not offered to everybody to bring things together into final focus. This suggests that we should try to become ever more conscious of the Lord in our lives, in our past as well as our present and future. Prayer should therefore be a regular and an important part of our daily routine. How ironic it would be if we were too busy to pray as we wanted for much of our life, and then neglected prayer when the opportunity for it was given to us. In prayer older persons cannot only lift up the needs of their dear ones. They can also reflect on the experience of their lifetime to discover how the Lord was at work there at every stage. Sometimes it is easier to see where the Lord was in our lives when we look at it from a certain distance. This kind of reflection should blossom into thanksgiving, into a kind of constant breathing of gratitude as we become aware of how much the Lord has done for us.

The opportunity to reflect in gratitude should also lead to

forgiveness. In every life there is pain, some of it inflicted on us by other people. Old age is a time to let go of our hurts, to commit them to the healing power of the Lord and to open our hearts in love to the persons who have harmed us, whether they are still with us or not.

But the prayerful reflectiveness of our final years need not be directed exclusively to the past. It can also be a time of new experience with the Lord, a time of discovery as we ponder the Lord's word in Scripture and come to know God in deeper ways. The God who has always been in our lives is still there, still inviting us to live and grow.

In addition to being open to receive what the Lord wants to give us, we should also be willing to share God's gifts with those around us. It is appropriate for those who have more time to use at least some of it in service to others: children, grandchildren, friends, service organizations. Our energy level may not be what it used to be, but there is generally *something* that we can do for somebody.

Moreover, an older person who lives in a state of increasing serenity in the Lord can be a source of great encouragement to younger people. Those who are young often wonder if there is any purpose in their lives. They need to be reassured that a life of faith is not a wasted life or a meaningless one. An older person who is willing to talk about the experiences of his or her life as it approaches its end can offer significant encouragement to the lives of others. Witnessing to our relationship with the Lord is not a task just for our years of greatest vigor.

Older men and women had a special role to play in the life of Jesus. John the Baptist, who was to prepare the way for Jesus' public life, was born of Zechariah and Elizabeth, chosen for their part in God's plan when they were well along in years. And when Jesus was presented in the temple, one of the few who were granted the privilege of recognizing him was Anna, a woman of prayer who was 84 years old.

Jesus tells us that he came so that we might have life and have it abundantly (see John 10:10). The kind of life that Jesus offers us is not merely the capacity to do things. It is also the capacity to receive. In fact, in the last analysis, it is when we are most willing to receive that we are most vigorously living in the Lord.

For Discussion

1) Explain why you look on old age as a burden or as a gift.

2) What opportunities do you think old age offers for living in the Lord?

3) What gifts have you received in life from older people?

Death:
The Final Fruitfulness

Death is a strange thing, filled with paradox.

All deaths are somehow the same, yet every death is unique. Every death is an ending, the conclusion of the physical existence of a physical creature. Every death is a release, the conclusion of the efforts and sufferings that are part of each human existence. Every death is sad, because every human life is good and the ending of any good thing carries with it an element of deprivation, of sadness.

Yet every death is unique because every person is unique. When a person dies, his or her specific blend of gifts and talents is taken from us, not to be replaced. It is not *some*one who dies, it is *this* one, this human being with his or her own history, capabilities, responsibilities, friendships, failures and achievements. What this person brought to the world is now over.

Death is common, yet death is rare. Every day there are several dozen death notices in the newspaper. In famine and earthquake hundreds or thousands of people die at one time. As we grow older, we experience the deaths of loved ones over and over again. Yet death is rare in the life of each individual. It only happens once. There is only one day in the life of each of us that does not bring the beginning of the next.

Death is known, yet death is unknown. We have known

73

people who have died; we know how and when they died. As we acquire experience we know what to say and do on the occasion of another's death. Yet death is unknown because none of us has yet shared the experience. It is unknown because none of us knows about our own death: when and how it will come or what it will be like.

In view of all that, we must learn the meaning of death—the death of others as well as our own. We must learn its place in living in the Lord.

Our Catholic Christian faith helps us come to grips with the dying that surrounds us and the death that awaits us. God has assured us in the resurrection of Jesus that, although death is real, although it is the last word of an earthly existence, it is also the first word of another kind of life. God's love for us is too great to allow us simply to stop being. Through death we go to God to begin a whole new level of being that has no end. Through death we enter a kind of being in which there is no pain, no suffering, no uncertainty, only fulfillment and joy in the eternal life of the Lord Jesus. Our Christian faith sees death neither as a simple reversion to nothingness nor as one step in a recurrent process of reincarnation, but as a once-and-for-all event that brings us to God forever.

This is not to say that our faith forbids us to grieve over the death of others. It is right to acknowledge the sense of loss that we feel when someone we knew and loved dies. The gap in our own life is real. The loss is real. The person who has died cannot be replaced by someone else. It is healthy to admit our sorrow and to prepare ourselves for the long process required for healing.

But at the same time, our Christian faith calls us to acknowledge that grief and loss is not all there is. After the death of a loved one there is still more—more for the one who has died and more for us. Death and grief are real, but so is God's care for those of us who remain behind and so is eternal life for the one who has died.

Coming to grips with the death of those around us helps us to come to terms with our own. Some people simply deny death and go on living as if there were no end. Others look on death with terror. God invites those who are living in the Lord to face death directly and realistically.

To be realistic about death means to admit to ourselves that our life here on earth will indeed come to an end. We may die quickly or slowly, we may be given some notice that our death is near or it may come to us unexpectedly. But die we shall. This is not to suggest that we should be afraid of death. We should be realistic, to be sure, but realism in the context of living in the Lord—and dying in the Lord—involves the assurance of God's concern and love for us human creatures.

God did not create us in order to be able to catch us out in a weak moment and then punish us. God created us for life, for life here and now and for life with Father, Son and Holy Spirit in the fullness of eternity. God invites us to grasp the life we have been given, our life in the Lord, to appreciate it, to enjoy it, to cultivate it, to put on it the imprint of our own individuality. Our life is a gift, an invitation to happiness, not a threat.

In death God brings the first stage of our existence to a close. When we die, God puts the finishing touch on what we and the Lord Jesus have become together. Death is the punctuation mark at the end of the story that we and Jesus have been writing throughout our life. Consequently, we should look on death not as some imposition from outside, but rather as the moment of final fruitfulness. In death God simply says to us, "It's time to stop working now. Let's enjoy what we have produced."

The quality of our death will be no different from the quality of our life. Because our life as Christians consists in the conscious and careful assimilation of the life of Christ, our death will necessarily involve a final and everlasting embrace into that life. In the tradition of Christian spirituality many saints have written on the art of dying well. Their common teaching is that the art of dying well consists in living well. Death is affirmation of that life, not denial.

As we live through our years on earth, then, it is important to keep ourselves aware of how well we are living. We need to take time out occasionally to look at our lives calmly and realistically. What is life all about? What is important to us? If the end of our earthly task were to come today, what would we have to show the Lord as our life's work?

Obviously there is sin in our life. But is our sinfulness something that we cling to because we are afraid of what might become of us if we gave it up, or is it something that we face up to and try to deal with? God doesn't leave us alone with our sins, but is there to forgive and to heal if we ask.

There are also missed opportunities in our life. We don't do everything that we could to cultivate the life of Christ in us. We don't reach out with Christ's love to others as generously as we might. Are we going to settle for this, or are we going to do something about it?

There may also be disappointment. Things haven't all turned out the way we had hoped. We haven't been able to do everything we wanted. Our achievements and successes are much smaller than our desires. But how important is all that? How much does it have to do with our main responsibility to live in the Lord?

We prepare ourselves best for death by paying attention to our lives. It's hard to be realistic about God's love for us, about how much we mean to God, about our life in the Lord if we never take time to look at what's going on.

We all face death, and we naturally feel a degree of fear. But we don't face death alone. Jesus is with us as we approach our end just as he was with us in our life. Jesus knows death. He wept over the death of his friend Lazarus (see John 11:35). He felt compassion for the widow of Naim when her son lay dead (see Luke 7:13). Jesus experienced death himself, a cruel and painful death. But it was not a death without meaning. In his dying Jesus brought to conclusion all that his life had been meant to be and handed over to the Father a mission fulfilled. When it comes time for us to die, if our life has been lived in the Lord, Jesus will be there to say in us and with us and for us, "Father, into your hands I commend my spirit" (Luke 23:46b).

For Discussion

1) How has your experience of the death of loved ones contributed to your living in the Lord?

2) What can you do today to get ready for death?

3) What would you like to leave behind for others when you die? What do you expect to take with you?

Liturgy:
Celebrating God's Love

In this book we have been considering the life and holiness that comes to us from God our Father through Jesus Christ, our Lord, by the working of the Holy Spirit. We have seen that our life and holiness are a freely given sharing in the life and the holiness of Christ, that our life is his life, that our spirituality is the carrying out in practice of the life and holiness of Christ which are already ours.

We saw that our life is shaped and directed and enlivened by God's gifts and by our response to them in faith, hope and love. We saw that friendship and family and work are contexts in which our relationship with the Lord finds particular expression. We saw that prayer is deliberate attentiveness to all this in the presence of God. We learned that life and holiness are also experienced in suffering, aging and even death.

A healthy Christian spirituality is one which helps us to remain aware in heart and in deed, in thought and in practice that there is no aspect of life that is foreign to Christ, no part of existence that is not rooted in his life and holiness.

Consequently, a healthy Christian spirituality is one which expresses itself in joy and gratitude and praise. As each of us becomes more and more conscious of who and what we are and are called to be in Christ, it is only natural to find ourselves saying,

"How strange and how wonderful that God should pay that kind of attention to me! Praise the Lord! Alleluia!"

At the same time, a healthy Christian spirituality will realize that there is no such thing as an exclusively "me and Jesus" relationship. God does not just relate to each of us individually, but always in the context of our sisters and brothers, who are loved as we are. The Church is the community of those who are bound together by the life and the holiness of Christ. We are one because we all share the one life and the one holiness of the one Christ.

Consequently, an appropriate response to the life and holiness of Christ can never be an exclusively individual response. The joy and gratitude and praise that we express as individuals must also be expressed with the others who share the life and holiness of Christ if our expression is to reflect the reality of our relationship with God.

All this is to say that Christian spirituality is directed toward celebration, toward the joyful acknowledgment of God's goodness in the company of those who share it. This is what heaven is all about: It is the full realization and complete expression of what we are in Christ, experienced in the company of the saints. Heaven is a party, a celebration that goes on forever.

But we don't have to wait for heaven to celebrate. We have an interim kind of celebration here and now in the context of the Church. It's called the liturgy. The liturgy is nothing less than the celebration of what we are and what we are to become in Christ and with Christ as the community of those who take part in his life, the Church.

Liturgy is complex because living in the Lord is complex. The Church invites us to rejoice and pray with Christ at every major moment of our lives, individual and corporate. In the sacraments the Church marks birth and maturity, the foundation of families and the provision of ministers for the Church. In the sacraments the Church rejoices over the return of the sinner and offers the compassion of Christ to its members at times of sickness and death. In the Eucharist, the liturgical act that we share in most frequently, the Church renews the self-giving of Christ and invites its members to unite themselves once more with him: with his life, his suffering, his death, his resurrection, his glory.

Because liturgy is the expression of what we are as well as what we are to be, it involves petition for our needs and sorrow for our sins along with thanks and praise. Because liturgy is prayer, it involves listening. Almost every liturgical action includes reading from the word of God as well as a homily, not to mention the sentiments that God awakens in our hearts as we place ourselves before God in prayer. A posture of receptivity is appropriate for every liturgical action.

Because liturgy is prayer, it also requires exertion. Each of us has our own contribution to make to the liturgy of the community. We contribute by making the effort to be present and give witness to the community of our own faith, hope and love. We also contribute to the liturgy by taking part in the singing and the common prayers. Then there is the interior effort of putting our hearts and minds in tune with the Church and with Christ as we offer together our praise and thanksgiving to our heavenly Father. If there is one attitude inappropriate for the liturgy, it is passivity.

That's because the center of all liturgy is celebration. In any celebration we acknowledge something good that has happened and take deliberate joy in it as a group. That's what we are called to do in the Church's worship: to reflect on and express what God has made us to be, to renew our awareness of God's presence in our lives through the love of the Lord Jesus, to enliven our confidence in God's action working through our activity and our relationships, to reawaken our hope in what God still has in store for us. The liturgy calls us to celebrate.

Why, then, does liturgy often seem so boring? Why do we go to Sunday Mass so often out of a sense of duty? Why does it seem that we get so little out of it?

We need to admit that often the celebration of the liturgy in our parishes is not everything it should be. Good liturgy doesn't just happen. It calls for preparation and for care in execution. It calls for a certain level of awareness in those who participate. Most parishes give considerable attention to the quality of their liturgical celebrations, but there is always room for improvement. If the liturgy in our parishes is not as good as we would like, perhaps the answer is not to complain but to offer ourselves to help make things better.

Sometimes liturgy isn't all it should be because of what we ourselves bring to it. If we come expecting to get an effortless spiritual "high," we will often be disappointed. Liturgy is not a wonder drug but an action for which we all share responsibility. We may find that liturgy means more to us if we consciously offer our own joys and sorrows, our own needs and achievements to the Lord with the priest and the community. Then the action becomes not just theirs, but ours as well.

People often find it helpful to take a little time before the liturgy to put their minds in the proper framework. Our lives are all busy and distracted; it's hard to shift from one context to another. That's why it's good to quiet ourselves before the liturgy and remind ourselves of what we have come to do.

And when the liturgy is over, we should not just walk out and take up where we left off. The celebration of the Church will mean much more to us if we try to take its spirit with us when we leave and plug into the rest of our life what we have experienced and expressed in church. Vatican II tells us that the liturgy is not just the goal toward which the Christian life is directed, but also the source from which its energy flows.

There is a wonderful passage in the Book of Revelation which deals with heaven:

> ...I heard what sounded like the loud voice of a great multitude in heaven, saying:
> "Alleluia!
> Salvation, glory, and might belong to our God....
>   Alleluia!
> The Lord has established his reign,
>   [our] God, the almighty.
> Let us rejoice and be glad
>   and give him glory." (Revelation 19:1, 6b—7a)

That celebration is the goal of living in the Lord. But even before that celebration begins for us, we are invited to celebrate with Christ and the Church in the liturgy. Even now the theme song of those who are living in the Lord is "Alleluia!"

For Discussion

1) Can we ever "celebrate" anything all by ourselves?

2) Why is liturgy important to living in the Lord?

3) What can you do to make participation in the liturgy more fruitful for yourself? For others?